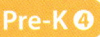

W0099588

Animals

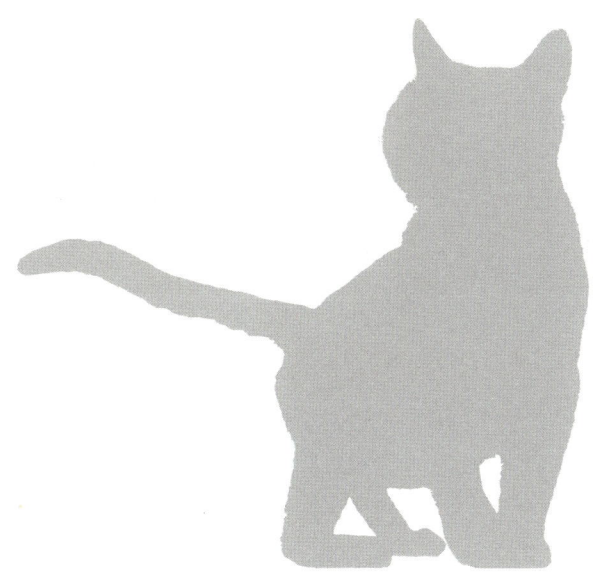

Seed Learning

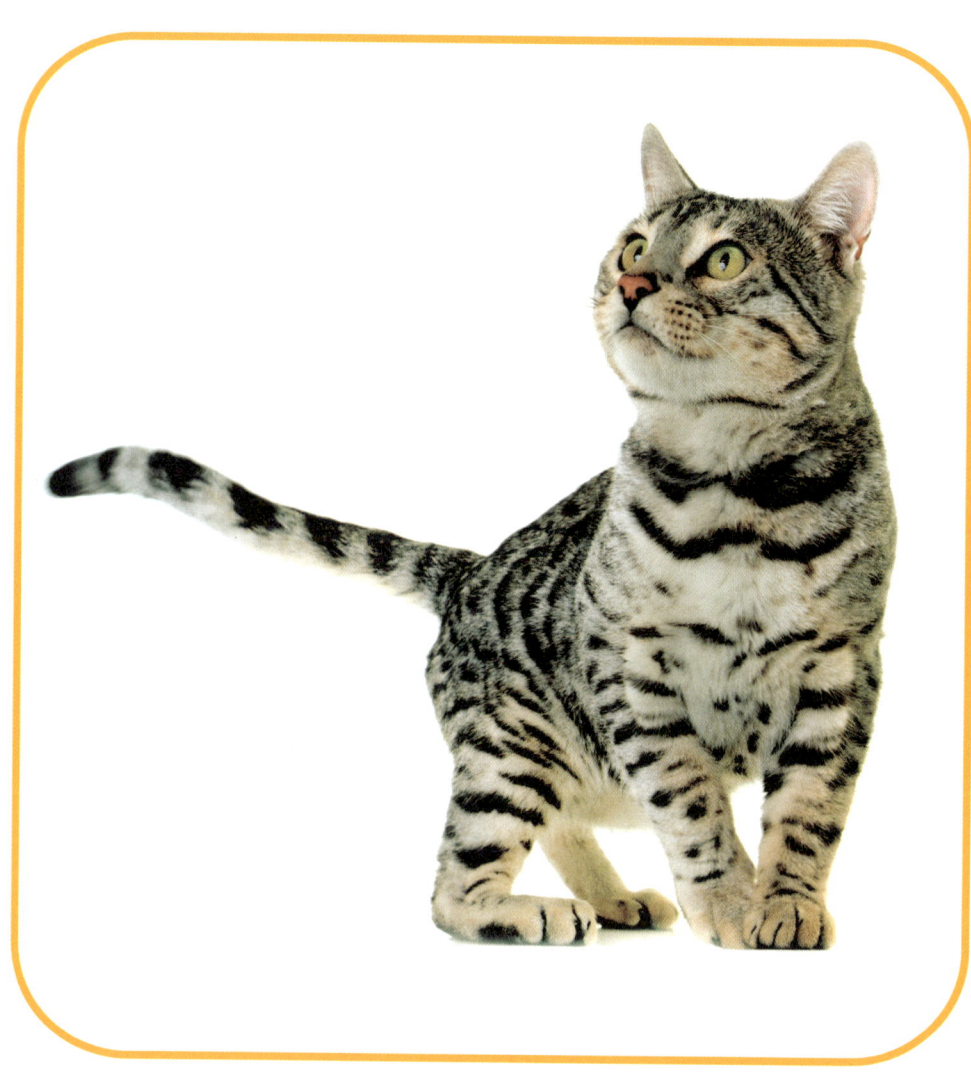

cat

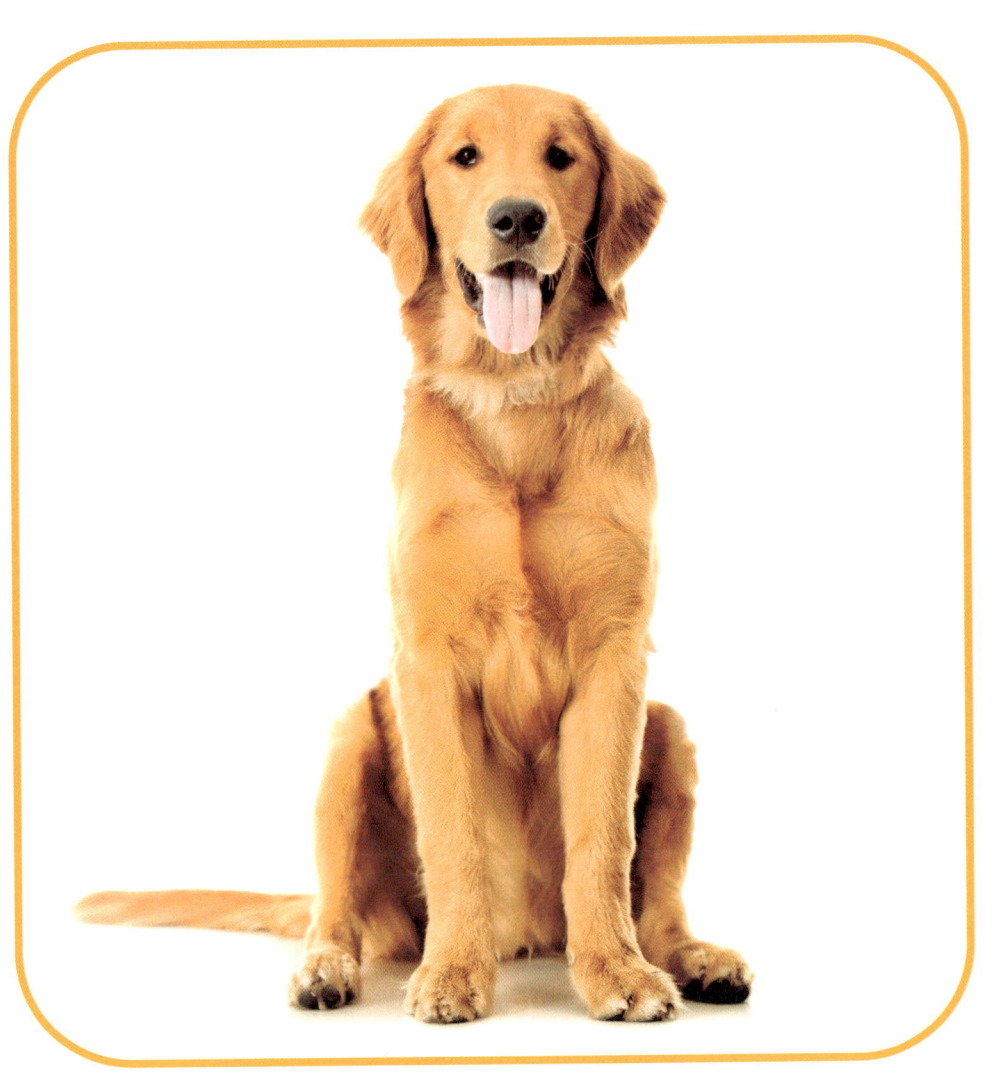

dog

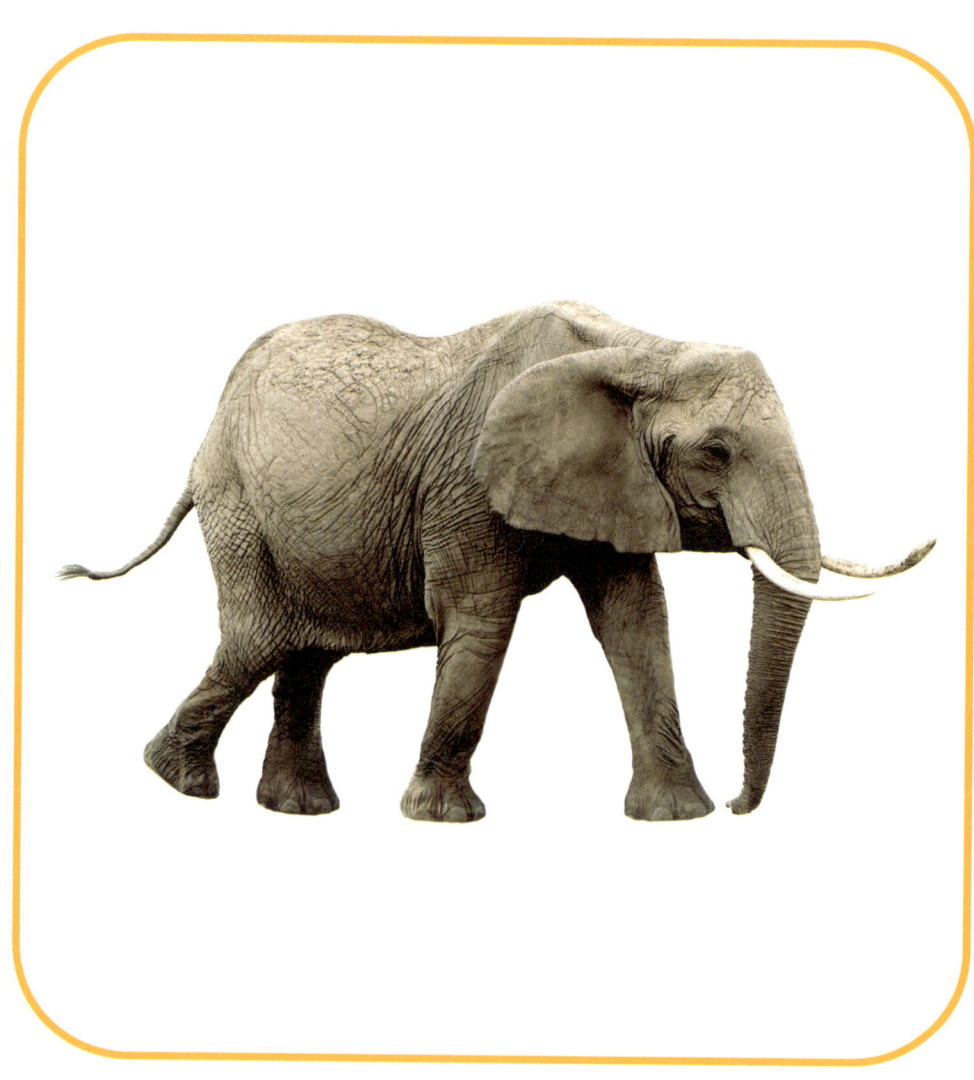

elephant

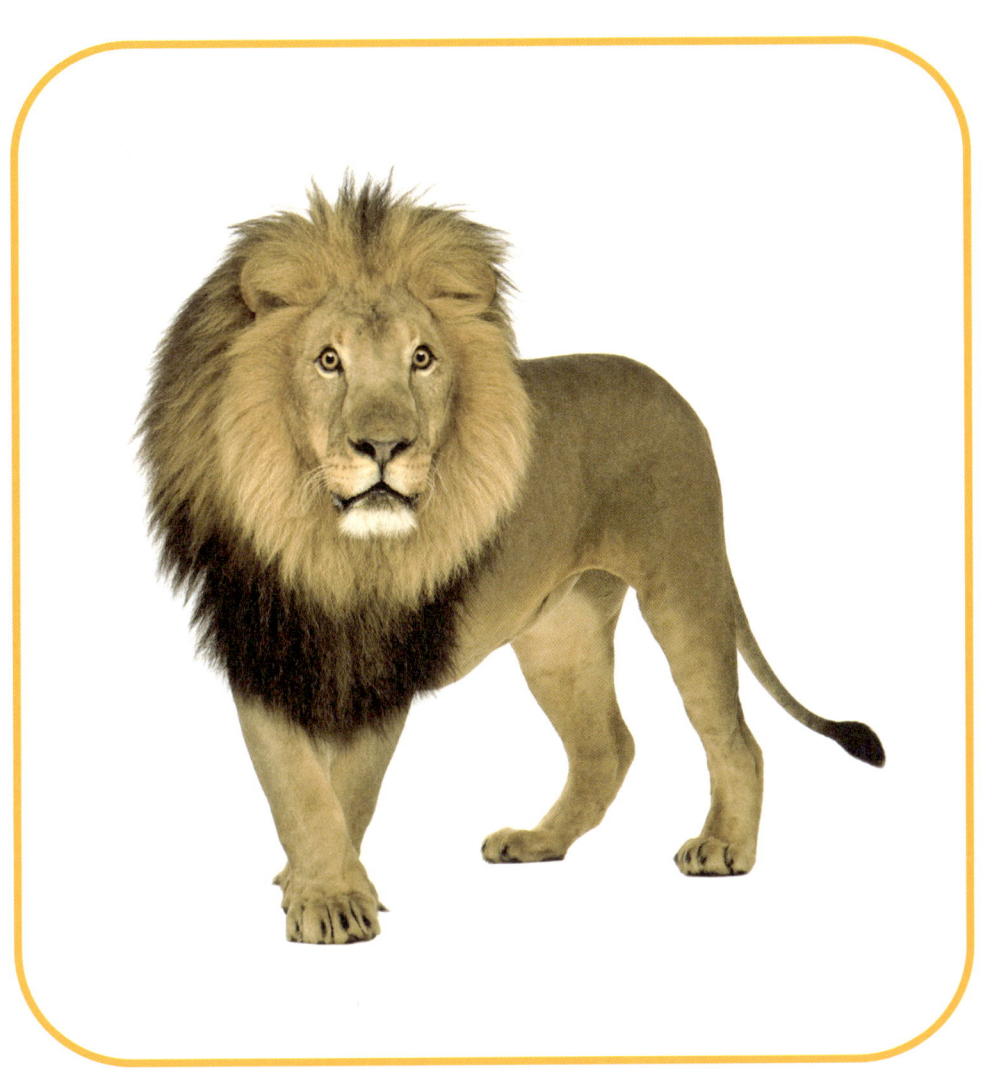

lion

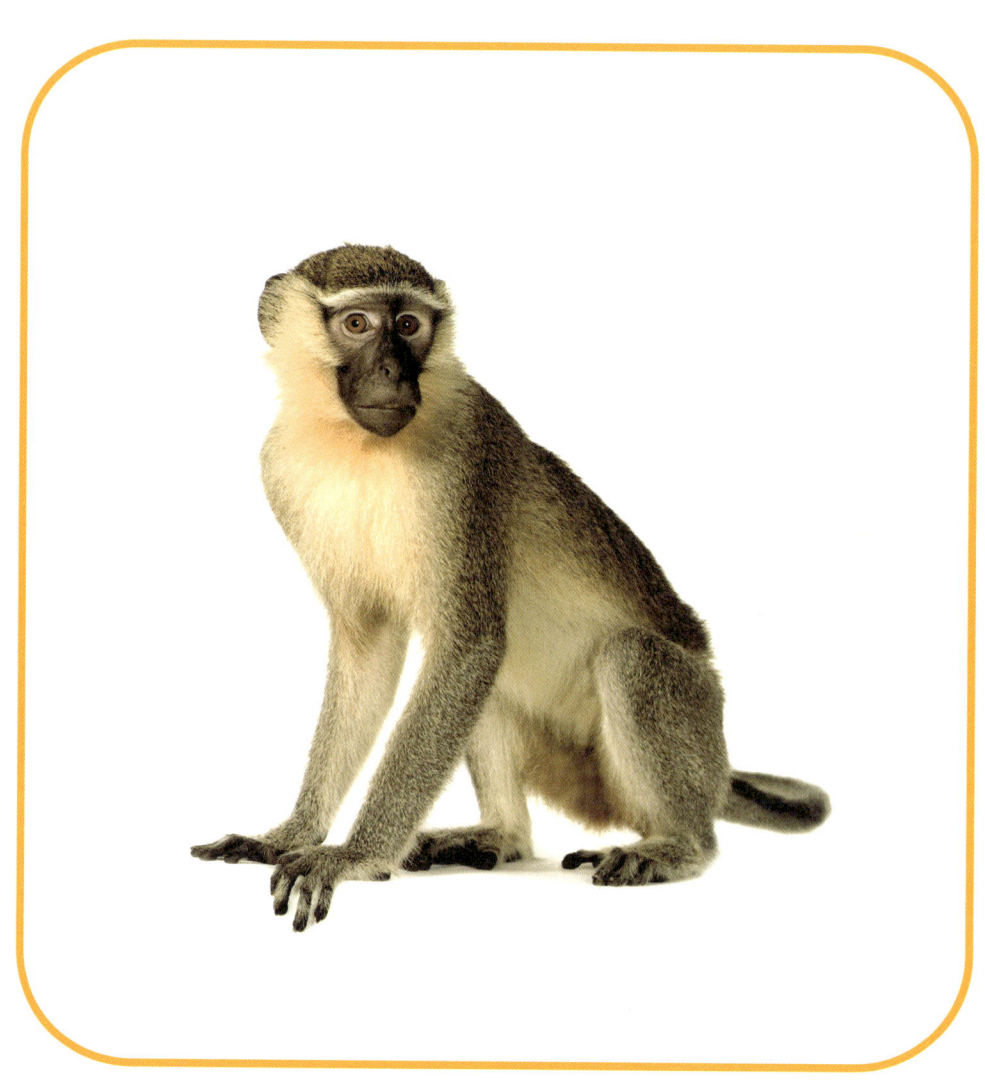

monkey

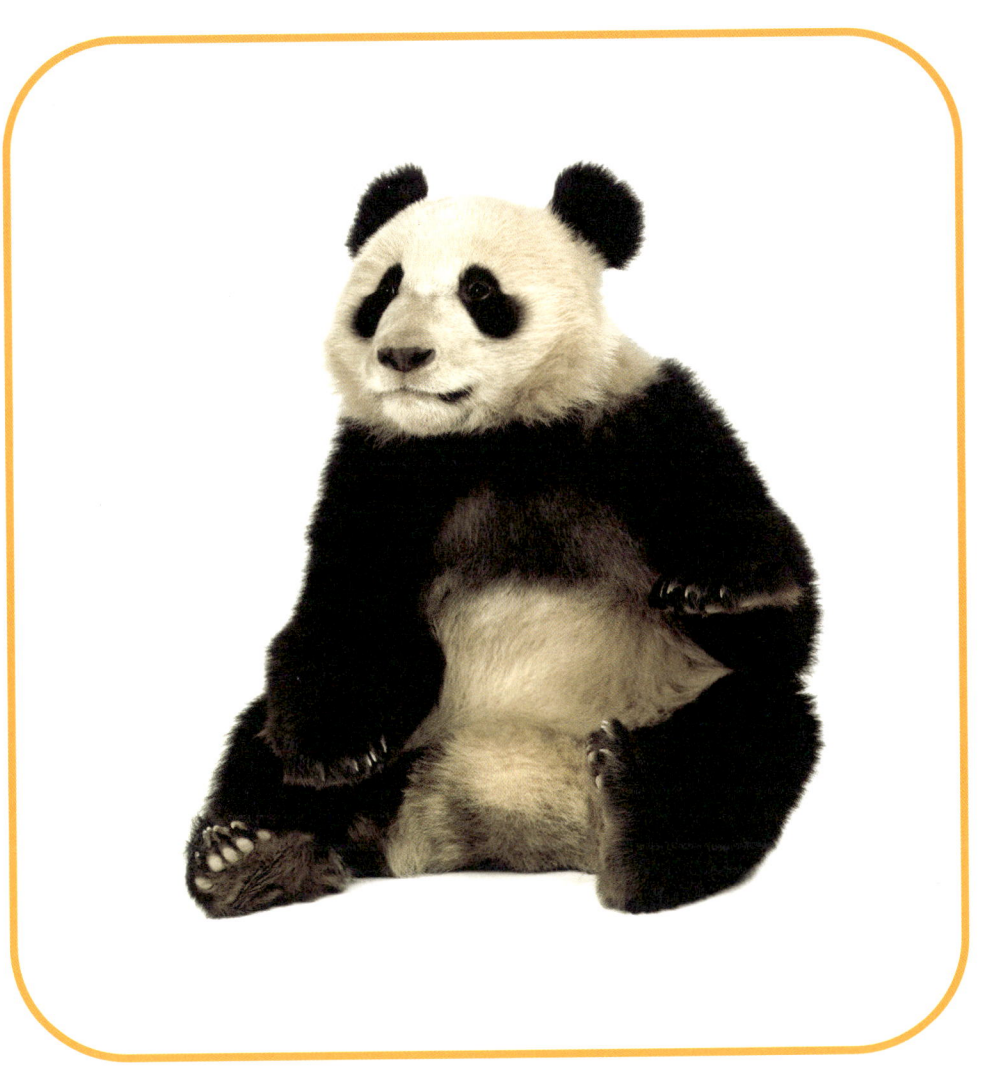

panda

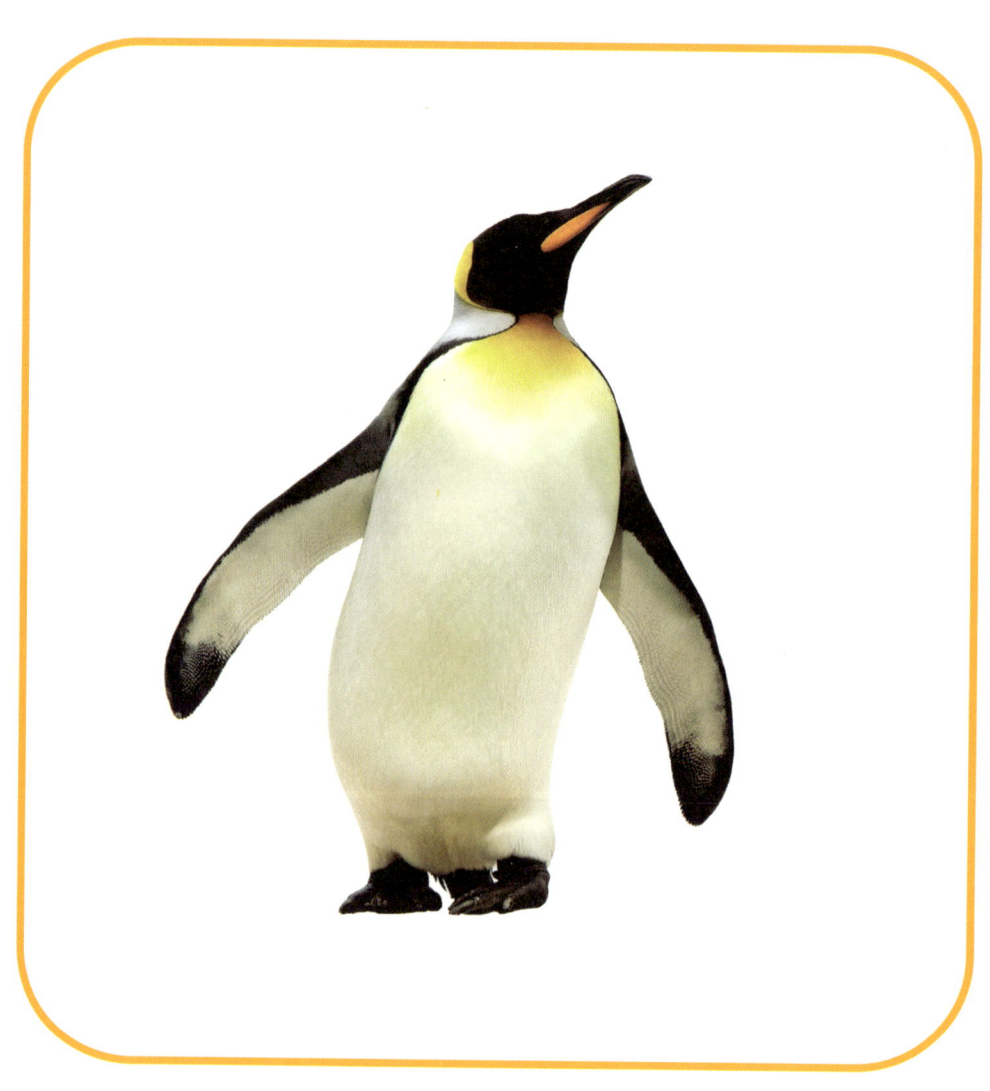

penguin

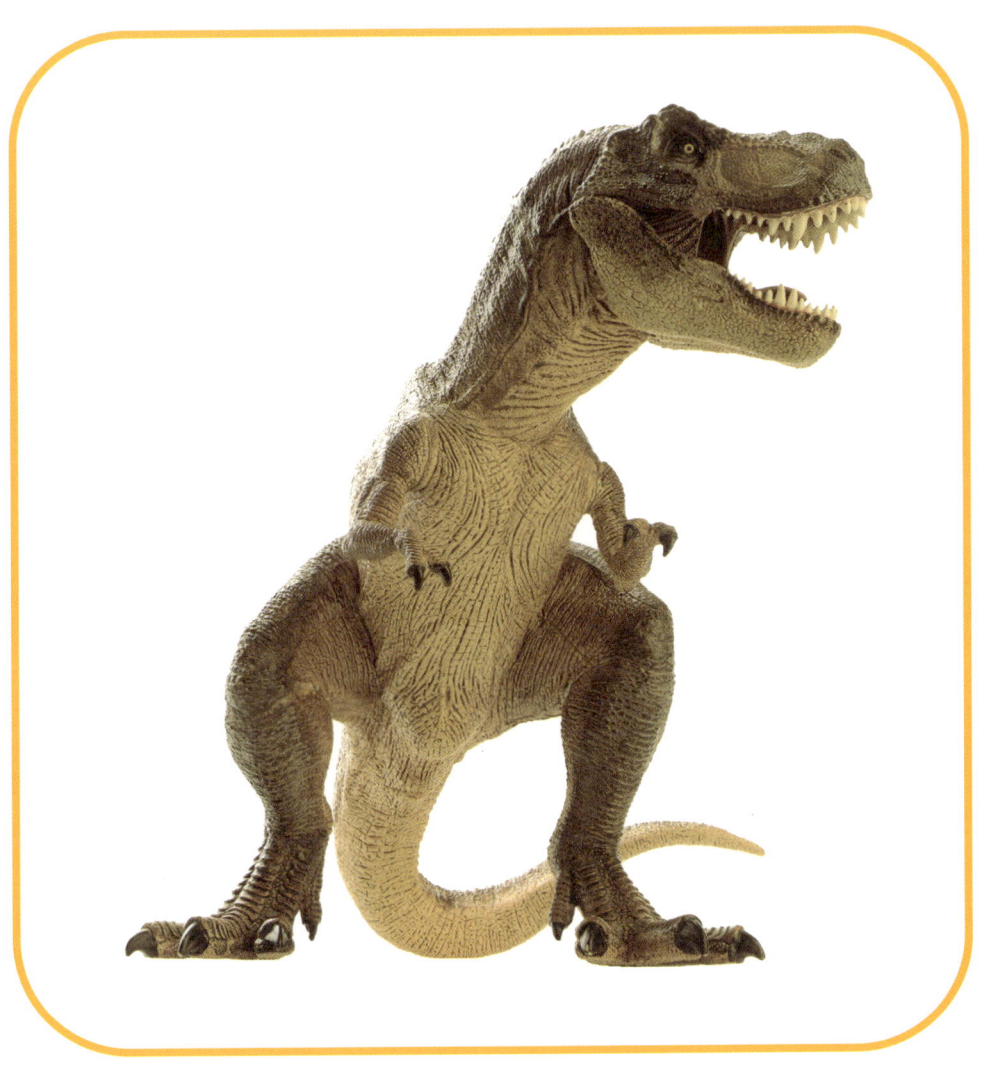

dinosaur

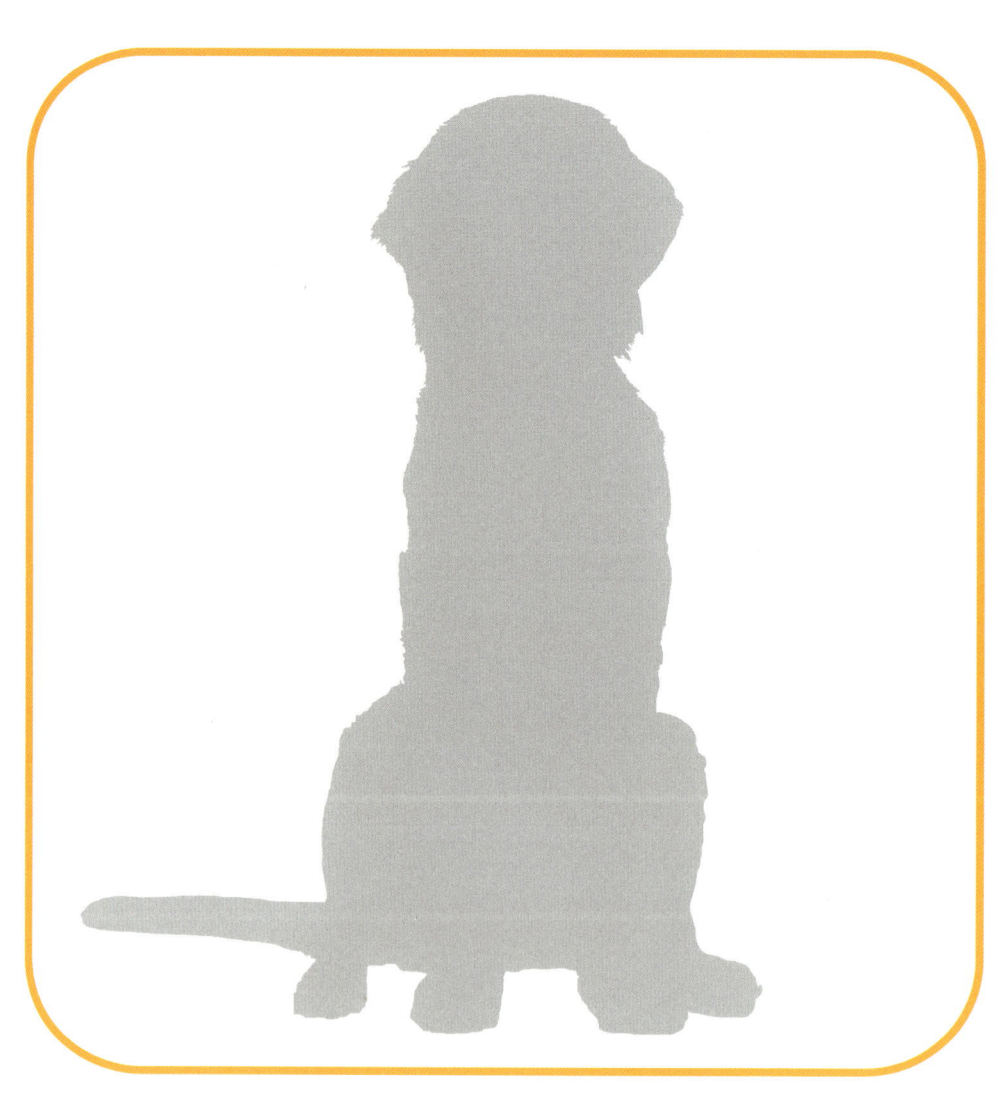

What is it?

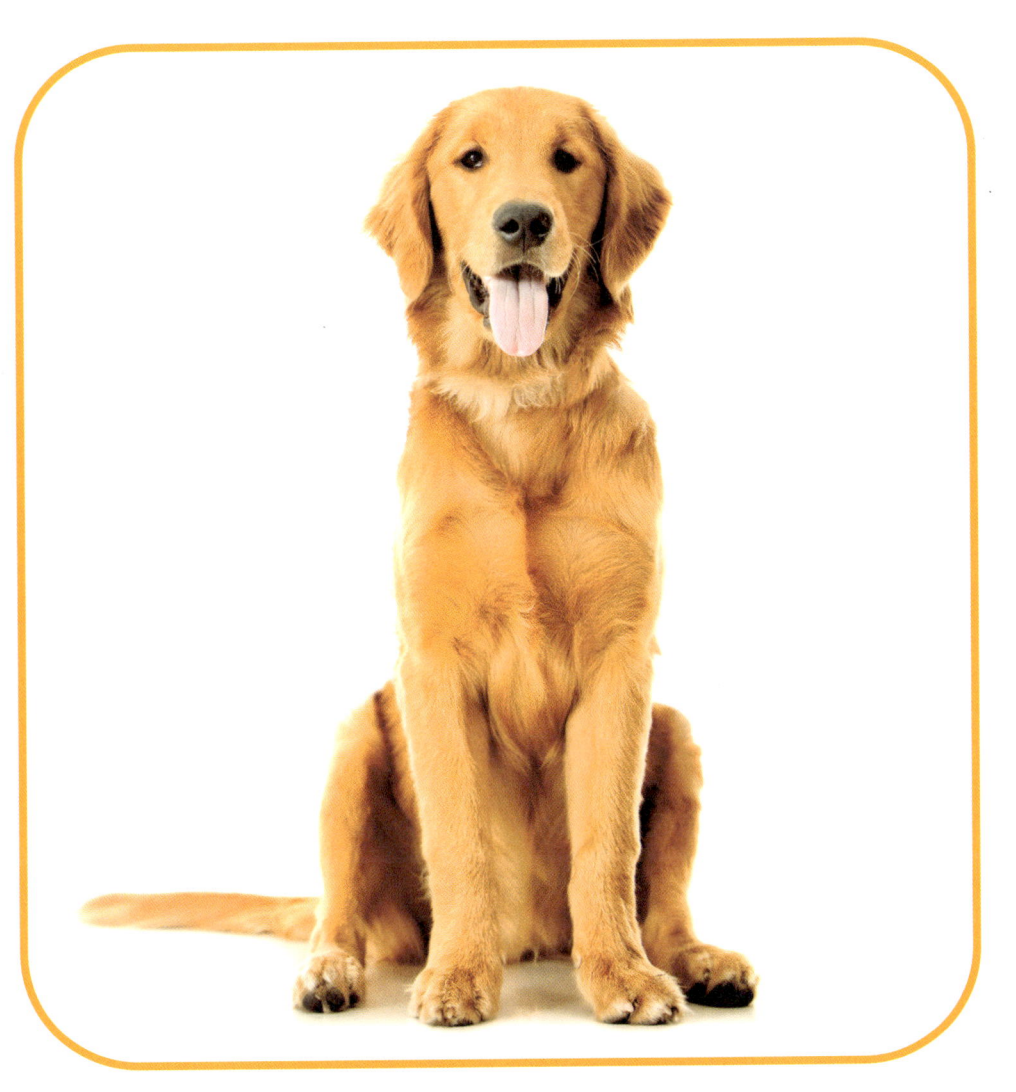

It's a dog.

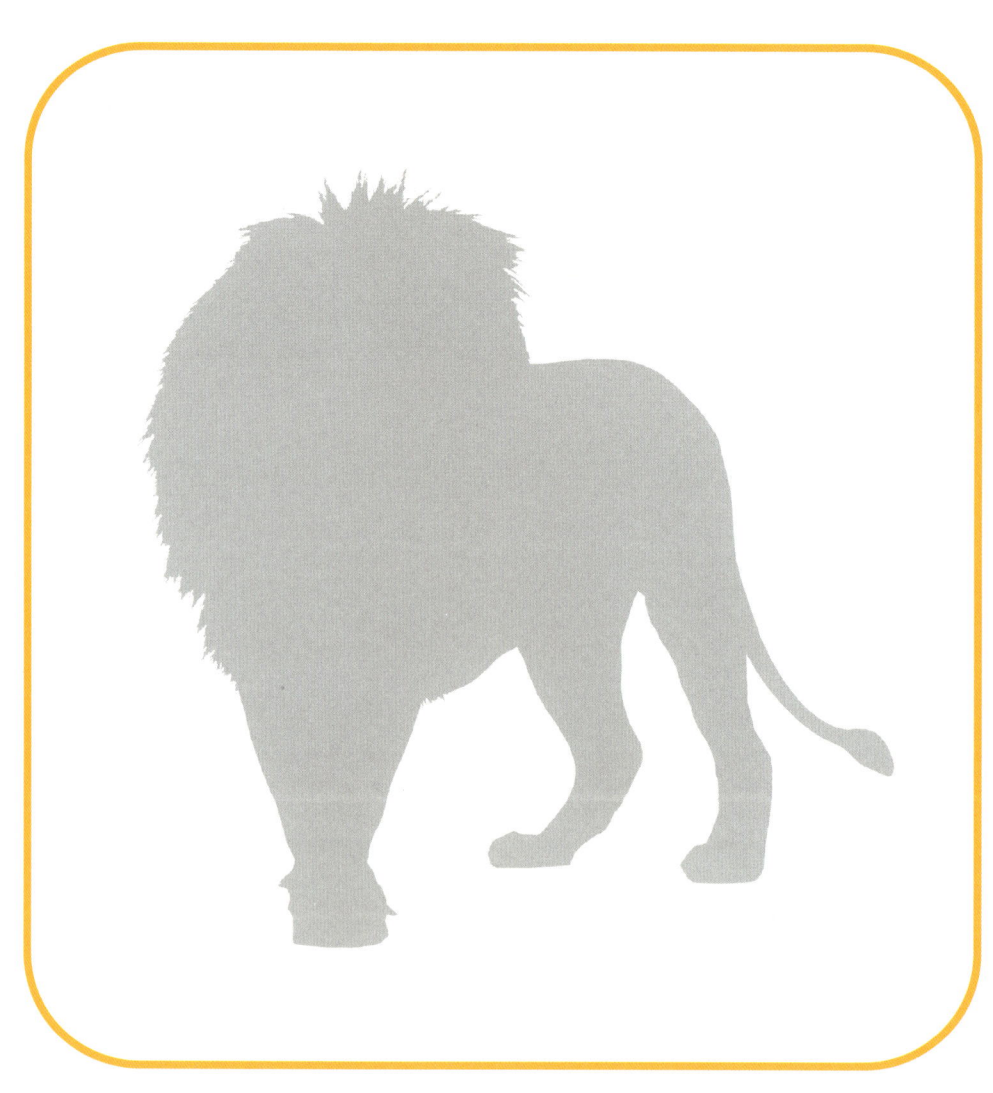

What is it?

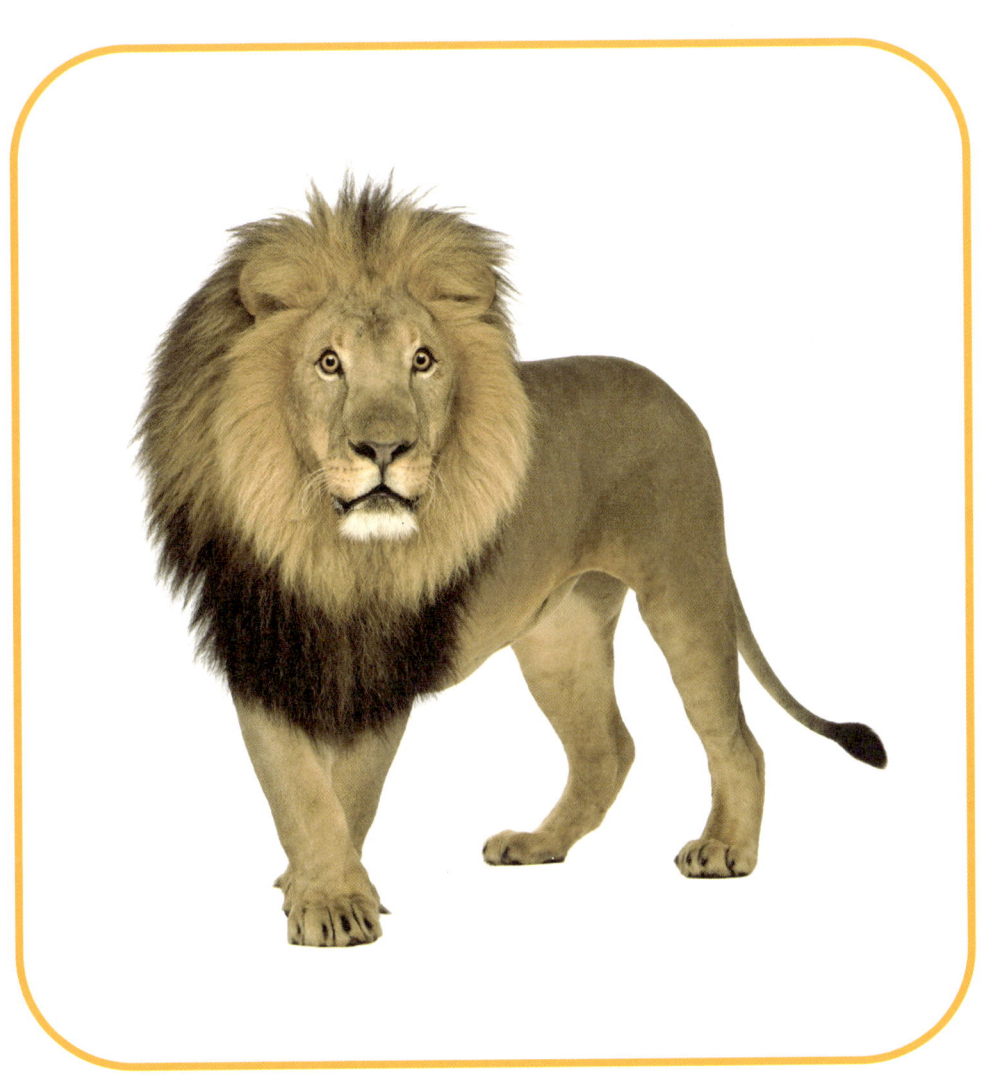

It's a lion.

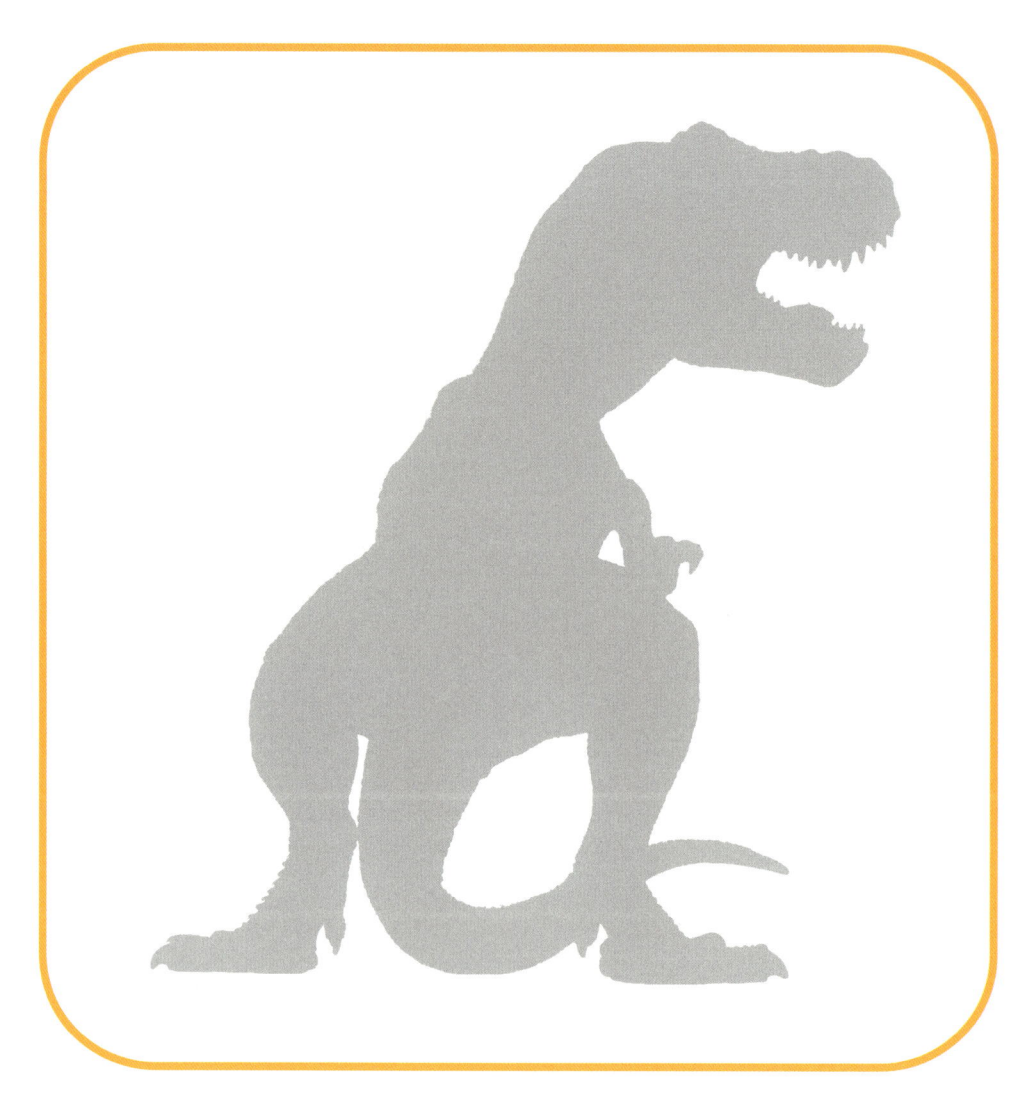

What is it?

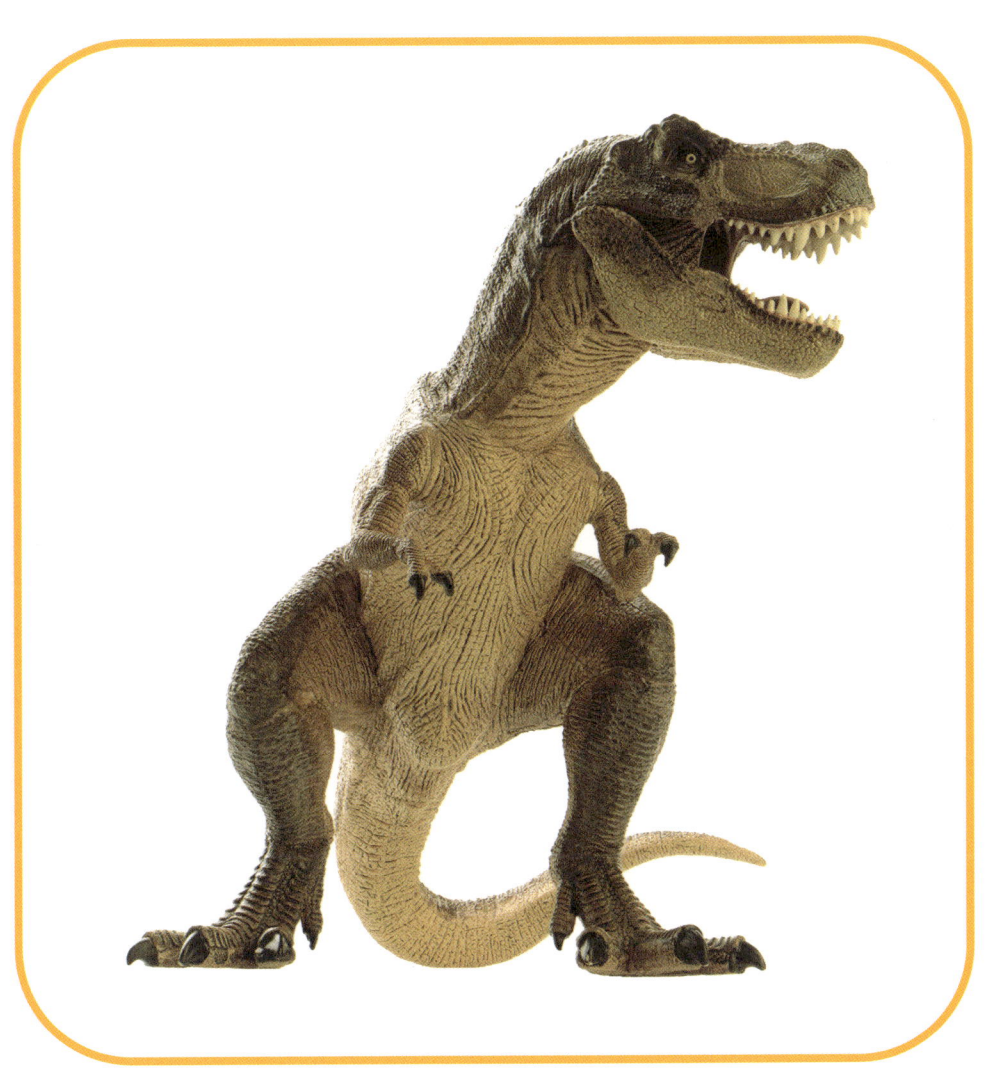

It's a dinosaur.

Word List

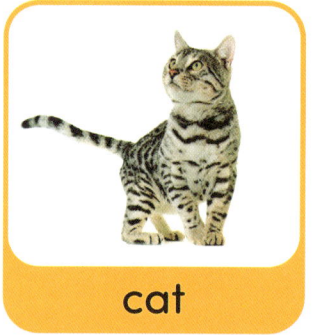

cat

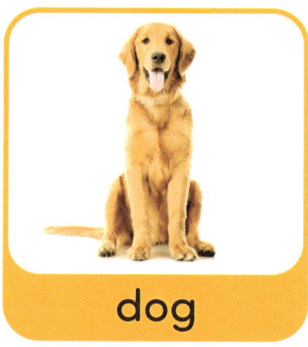

dog

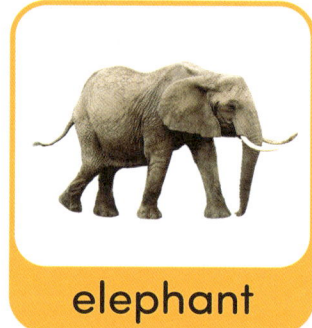

elephant

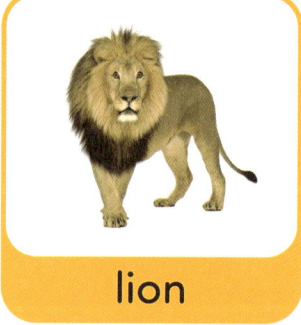

lion

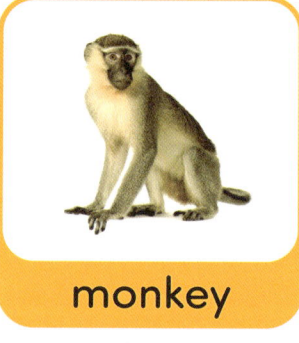

monkey

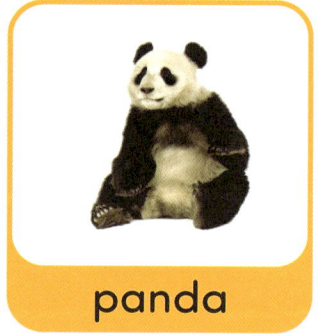

panda

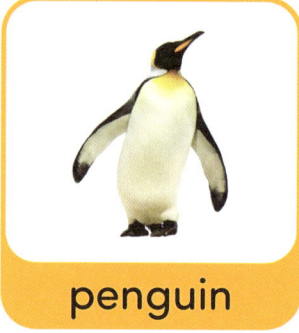

penguin

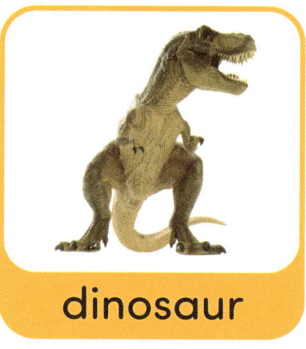

dinosaur